In the
DARK

THE SCIENCE OF WHAT HAPPENS AT NIGHT

LISA DERESTI BETIK · JOSH HOLINATY

KIDS CAN PRESS

For Noah and Will, whose curiosity makes life wild and wonderful — LDB

Acknowledgments

I'm grateful for all of the kind people at Kids Can Press, especially my editors, Kathleen Keenan and Yasemin Uçar, who so skillfully helped me create this exciting first book. Thank you to the talented Josh Holinaty, whose brilliant illustrations light up its pages. I'd like to acknowledge expert reviewers Dr. Tammy Jechura, Dr. Scott Ramsay, Dr. Sheila Lyons-Sobaski and Dr. Nicolle Zellner for their thoughtful comments and interesting contributions to the text. Heartfelt thanks to my family, especially Matt, Noah and Will, for their love, support and enthusiasm throughout this project and always.

Text © 2020 Lisa Deresti Betik
Illustrations © 2020 Josh Holinaty

Kids Can Press gratefully acknowledges the financial support of the Government of Ontario, through Ontario Creates; the Ontario Arts Council; the Canada Council for the Arts; and the Government of Canada for our publishing activity.

Published in Canada and the U.S. by
Kids Can Press Ltd.
25 Dockside Drive, Toronto, ON M5A 0B5

Kids Can Press is a Corus Entertainment Inc. company

www.kidscanpress.com

The artwork in this book was rendered digitally. The text is set in Open Sans.

Edited by Yasemin Uçar and Kathleen Keenan
Designed by Barb Kelly

Printed and bound in Shenzhen, China, in 3/2020 by C & C Offset

CM 20 0 9 8 7 6 5 4 3 2 1

FSC
MIX
Paper from responsible sources
FSC® C008047
www.fsc.org

Library and Archives Canada Cataloguing in Publication

In the dark : the science of what happens at night / Lisa Deresti Betik ; Josh Holinaty.

Deresti Betik, Lisa, 1972– author. | Holinaty, Josh, 1983– illustrator.

Includes bibliographical references and index.

Canadiana 20190215585 |
ISBN 9781525301094 (hardcover)

LCSH: Night — Juvenile literature. | LCSH: Science — Juvenile literature.

LCC Q163 .D47 2020 | DDC j508 — dc23

TABLE OF CONTENTS

WHAT HAPPENS
after Dark?

In the evenings, as the sky grows dark, living creatures of all different shapes and sizes prepare themselves for sleep. You might enjoy a bedtime snack, put on a favorite pair of pajamas, brush your teeth and settle into bed to read by the light of a softly glowing lamp. Before long, your eyes are closed and you're drifting off to dreamland. Have you ever wondered, though, what might be happening while you're asleep?

There's a whole world of exciting activity happening during the dark hours of the night. The human brain and body may seem quiet, but they're actually performing many important tasks that keep us healthy. Some living creatures are most active during nighttime hours. They use their specially adapted features, such as large eyes or a strong sense of smell, to help them find food in the relative safety of the dark. Even plants are active after the sun sets! Scientists have discovered that plants do a kind of math inside their leaves at night, and there are several species that bloom only under moonlight. Above us all, the night sky is full of faraway, brightly glowing objects that have long inspired humans to learn more about the universe.

If you've ever been curious about the wild and wonderful things that happen while you sleep, turn the page and discover the magic of the world after dark.

Sleep UNCOVERED

In 1964, an American teenager named Randy Gardner wanted to do something exciting for his science fair project. He decided to try to break the Guinness World Record for staying awake the longest, which meant going without any sleep at all for *11* whole days and nights. (If you've ever tried to stay awake for one night at a sleepover, you'll know what Randy was getting himself into!)

Randy didn't find the first couple of sleepless nights too difficult. Friends helped him stay alert by playing games and sports with him, talking to him and encouraging him to take cold showers when he needed to perk up. But the longer Randy stayed awake, the more he began to struggle.

Randy managed to break the world record — and win the science fair — by staying awake for 264 straight hours (amazing)! More important, though, Randy's experiment helped scientists confirm just how necessary sleep is for humans. While we're sleeping, our bodies and brains perform tasks that help us function at our best while we're awake.

So how exactly does sleep work? What's really going on, on the inside, when we appear mostly still and quiet on the outside?

Lights Out

Guinness World Records no longer keeps track of the longest time spent awake. Because long periods of sleeplessness can be dangerous for humans, Guinness didn't want to encourage other people to try the same experiment Randy did.

His eyelids grew heavy.

He experienced blurry vision that made it hard to read or watch television.

Interesting!

He became cranky and didn't want to cooperate.

He had trouble speaking.

He grew clumsier and more and more forgetful.

Hello, Randy.

Mom?

He even started seeing things that weren't actually there.

Tick, Tock: OUR BIOLOGICAL CLOCK

You probably wear a watch or carry a device that tells time. Like other living creatures, you also have a biological, or built-in, clock that helps determine when you should be awake and when you should be asleep. This natural programming of your body is known as a **circadian** (sir-CAY-dee-an) **rhythm**. In the same way that Earth rotates on its axis once every 24 hours, your body follows a 24-hour cycle of waking and sleeping.

Your brain contains a group of nerve cells called the **suprachiasmatic nucleus** (soo-prah-KY-as-MAT-ic NOO-clee-us), or SCN, located between and behind your eyes. The SCN picks up clues about light and dark from the retina, a thin layer of tissue at the back of your eye that receives light and sends electrical signals to your brain. The SCN sends messages to other parts of your brain and body to coordinate the timing of important tasks such as eating, sleeping and producing **hormones**.

When it grows dark outside, the SCN tells your body to release melatonin, a hormone that helps you feel drowsy. The melatonin levels in your body are ten times higher at night than they are during the day.

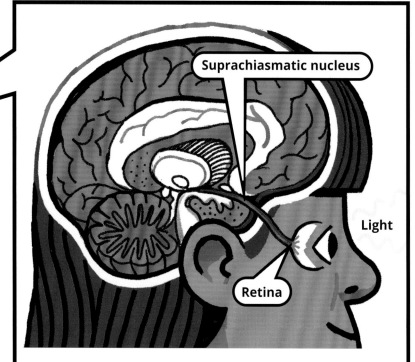

Suprachiasmatic nucleus

Light

Retina

When the SCN detects daylight reaching your retina, it sends messages to let your body know it's *go* time! Your temperature rises and your body releases a hormone called cortisol, which makes you alert.

TOO TIRED

If you've ever traveled to a different time zone, you've probably noticed your own circadian rhythm. Did you feel tired, foggy headed or grouchy as you adjusted to the new day and night schedule? This experience is called jet lag, and it happens because the human body needs several days, or sometimes weeks, to reset its internal clock.

People who work night shifts, such as hospital and hotel workers, police officers, pilots and truck drivers, might also find the changes to their normal sleep patterns challenging. Shift workers must find a way to sleep during sunlight hours and be awake and alert when it's dark outside. Earplugs and room-darkening curtains might help with daytime sleep, while eating well and staying active at work might encourage nighttime alertness.

Sleep, IN STAGES

Sleeping seems simple enough: we rest with our eyes closed, mostly unaware of what's happening around us. But a closer look reveals just how lively our brains and bodies are after dark.

Humans cycle through several stages of sleep during the night. There are three different stages of non-rapid eye movement (NREM) sleep and one stage of rapid eye movement (REM) sleep.

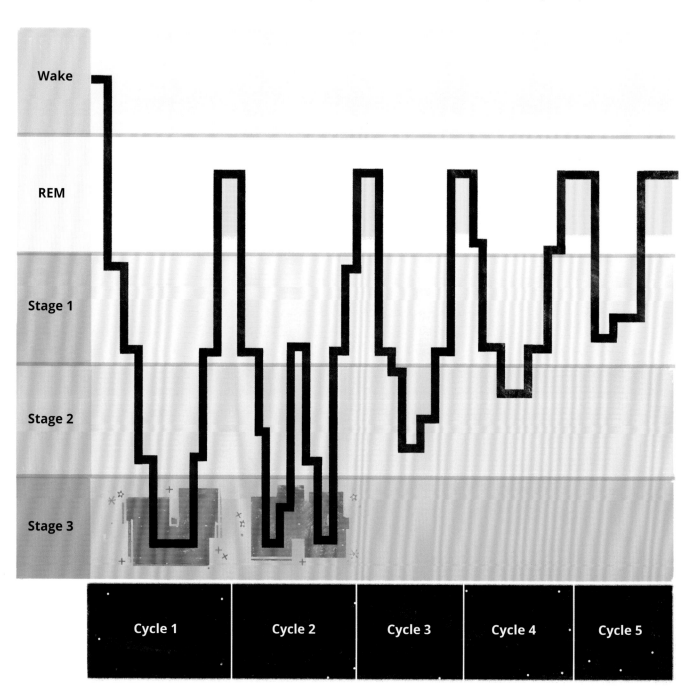

	Wake
	REM
	Stage 1
	Stage 2
	Stage 3

Sleep activity   **Deep sleep**   **Dreams**

Cycle 1   Cycle 2   Cycle 3   Cycle 4   Cycle 5

Stage 1: NREM Sleep (less than 10 minutes)

- short stage of dozy, light sleep
- breathing is regular
- heart rate and brain activity slow down
- muscles are still active (eyes may slowly roll and bodies may suddenly twitch or jolt)

Stage 2: NREM Sleep (10 to 25 minutes)

- light sleep
- breathing and heart rate slow down and body temperature drops
- brain activity continues to slow down, with some bursts of faster activity
- muscle activity lessens

Stage 3: NREM Sleep (20 to 40 minutes)

- deepest sleep (waking is difficult)
- body temperature and blood pressure lower
- breathing rate and heart rate slow down further
- stage when sleepwalking is most likely to occur

Stage 2: NREM Sleep (5 to 10 minutes)

- brief return to lighter sleep

REM Sleep (about 10 minutes)

- closed eyes move quickly and randomly from side to side
- fast, shallow, irregular breathing
- heart rate and blood pressure rise
- brain uses lots of oxygen
- small, high-frequency brain waves suggest a lot of concentrating and thinking
- stage when most dreams occur (especially longer, vivid ones)

One complete sleep cycle goes through all of these stages and lasts about 50 to 90 minutes. The cycle generally repeats itself four to six times a night. In the night's earlier cycles, we spend more time in Stage 3 NREM, our deepest sleep. In the later cycles, we spend more time in REM sleep.

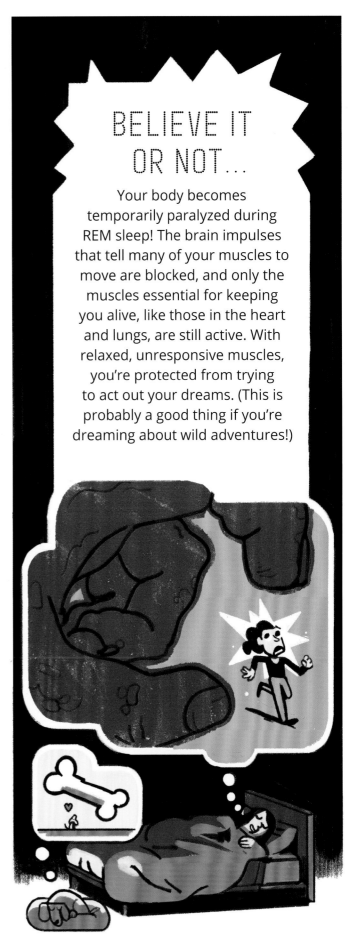

BELIEVE IT OR NOT...

Your body becomes temporarily paralyzed during REM sleep! The brain impulses that tell many of your muscles to move are blocked, and only the muscles essential for keeping you alive, like those in the heart and lungs, are still active. With relaxed, unresponsive muscles, you're protected from trying to act out your dreams. (This is probably a good thing if you're dreaming about wild adventures!)

WHY DO *We Sleep?*

Sleep was once thought to be a time when our bodies and brains "turned off" to allow us to rest and recharge. Now scientists understand that sleep involves much more than that.

Sleep allows our brains to file away new information.

Our brains record all kinds of information when we're awake. During sleep, our brains process this information, deciding which parts to combine with other information and file away for future use. Studies show that we perform better on memory tasks when we sleep after learning. (So it might not be a good idea to stay up all night studying for a test — you need sleep to hold on to that material!)

Sleep regulates the release of hormones.

Hormones are chemical substances that control what certain cells or organs do. Our bodies release growth hormone primarily during deep sleep. This hormone is important for both children and adults because it repairs and maintains our tissues.

Sleep also helps our bodies maintain an ideal level of insulin. Insulin is the hormone that controls our blood sugar levels and allows our cells to get energy from glucose, a form of sugar that comes from food. The hunger hormones ghrelin, which makes us feel hungry, and leptin, which signals when we're full, are also regulated by sleep. When we don't get enough sleep, our hunger hormones become unbalanced and we might eat more than we need to.

Sleep lets our brains do some cleaning.

Using powerful microscopes that can see through a person's skull, scientists have noticed that cells in our brains shrink at night. The spaces left between the cells allow the brain to clean itself during sleep. How? The brain is surrounded by a sac filled with fluid that protects it. At night, this fluid flows through the entire brain, washing away waste particles. (If only your room would clean itself, too!)

Changing PATTERNS

Our bodies grow and change over time, so our sleep needs change, too. Babies' brains and bodies are so busy developing that they need about 16 to 20 hours of sleep a day. But by the time those babies are teenagers, they'll only need about 8 to 10 hours of sleep each night. Our sleep patterns continue to shift even in adulthood. Most people will spend about one-third of their lives asleep. By the time you're 75 years old, 25 of your years will have been spent snoozing.

BABIES' short sleep cycles last about 60 minutes, and they fall into REM sleep first.

YOUNG CHILDREN (between ages 4 and 10) spend more time in Stage 3 NREM deep sleep than adults do.

ELDERLY ADULTS experience fewer, shorter periods of deep sleep interrupted by periods of wakefulness.

From about age 20 on, **ADULTS** generally need 7 to 9 hours of sleep a night.

TEENAGERS experience a shift in their circadian rhythms that makes it feel natural for them to stay up later at night and sleep in till later in the morning.

What a SNORE!

When you sleep, the muscles at the back of your mouth and throat relax. The tissues in that area become so soft they can vibrate when air passes through them, creating a rattling noise — snoring! Snoring can also be caused by a relaxed tongue falling toward the back of your throat or swollen upper-airway tissues from a cold or allergies. About 20 percent of adults snore regularly. (Earplugs, anyone?)

Some snorers raise the head of their bed or learn to play a wind instrument like a flute or trumpet to strengthen their throat muscles. Others sew a tennis ball to the back of their pajamas! When rolling on their backs is uncomfortable, they're more likely to sleep on their sides and keep their airways clear.

Midnight ADVENTURES

Some people, especially children, get up and wander while deeply asleep! Sleepwalking, or **somnambulism** (som-NAM-byuh-liz-um), happens when someone gets out of bed without realizing and moves around unpredictably. Sleepwalkers sometimes move furniture, cook or even climb out a window. Their eyes are open but unfocused, and if you wake them, they'll seem confused.

What's in a DREAM?

Do you remember your dreams? We all dream multiple times a night, whether we remember it or not. Most people will spend more than 52 000 hours of their lives dreaming! But dreaming is a subject that scientists are still exploring. In general, dreams reflect our everyday lives. We usually dream about people and places we know and the same kinds of things we think about and experience when we're awake. Dreams may help us strengthen our memories and manage our emotions.

But what about those vivid, bizarre dreams we have? When we're dreaming, the **limbic system** — the "feeling and reacting" part of our brains — is working in high gear. But some areas of the **prefrontal cortex** — the "reasoning, logical, planning" part of our brains — are less active during sleep. This makes our dreams colorful and emotional, but the events that happen in them may be disconnected and may not seem to make much sense.

Making SENSE OF IT ALL

Many scientists believe that dreams help our brains figure out what the events of our day mean. As we dream, our stored-up daily memories flow from the hippocampus (hip-puh-CAM-pus) to the neocortex, where they are connected to other memories. Our brains use dreams to see how our experiences fit together.

Dreaming may also help us develop strategies to use in future challenges when we're awake. In one experiment, a group of people went through a maze. Half the people then had a nap, while the others stayed awake. Later, the people who had napped *and* dreamed about the maze were able to find the exit ten times faster than the non-nappers!

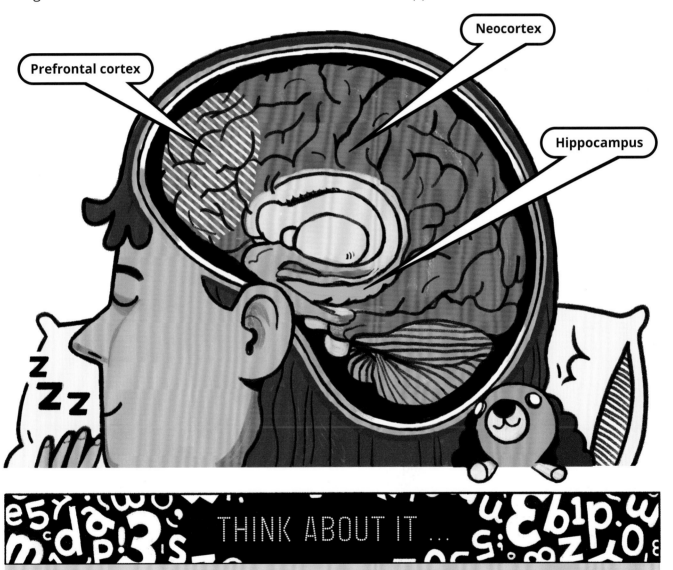

Neocortex

Prefrontal cortex

Hippocampus

THINK ABOUT IT ...

Studies show that we rarely dream about activities such as reading, writing, calculating or using a computer. We might open a book in a dream, but our brains will have a hard time creating the words. It's also difficult for our brains to change lighting conditions in our dreams. Have you ever dreamed about lights going on or off?

NOCTURNAL Creatures

Each evening, as humans slip under the covers, many other creatures are just beginning to stir. **Nocturnal** species come out at night from the secret places where they've spent their day sleeping. They run and fly, hunt and forage, and build and pollinate under inky skies speckled with stars.

Creatures that are most active at night are called nocturnal, while those most active during the day are called **diurnal** (dye-UR-nul). **Crepuscular** (cre-PUS-cue-lur) creatures are most active during twilight hours, just after the sun rises (dawn) and just before it sets (dusk).

IT'S ALL ABOUT ADAPTATION

An **adaptation** is a genetic change passed down from one generation to the next that helps an animal survive in its environment. Through adaptation, nocturnal creatures have developed some special abilities to see, hear, smell, sense or even glow in the dark!

Why are some creatures most active at night?

Some creatures, such as spring peepers, hide when it's light out to avoid being seen by daytime predators.

Some predatory animals hunt at night because their prey is most active in the dark. Darkness also gives leopards, wolves and other hunting creatures a chance to sneak up on their prey.

For some creatures, being nocturnal means facing less competition with others for food, water, space and shelter. (Owls, for example, can hunt for mice at night without encountering hawks, who seek out mice during the day.)

Thanks to cooler nighttime temperatures in dry desert climates, nocturnal creatures, such as fennec foxes, can be active without getting too hot or becoming dehydrated.

IN THE DEEP DARK SEA

Did you know that the largest animal migration on our planet happens after dark? Every night, trillions of sea creatures that travel in groups called schools — fish, shrimp, krill, squid, jellyfish and copepods — swim up from deep waters toward the ocean's surface to feed on plankton. These creatures return to deeper water before sunrise to avoid predators who hunt by day.

NIGHT *Vision*

Have you ever heard your cat darting around at night and wondered how she sees in the dark? Cats' eyes and human eyes share some similarities. When light reaches the retina at the back of the eye, it is received by two types of cells called rods and cones. These cells send signals to the brain through the optic nerve.

Cones detect colors and fine details in bright light

Rods register shapes and movement in dim light

Tapetum lucidum cells reflect light particles that have already passed through the retina

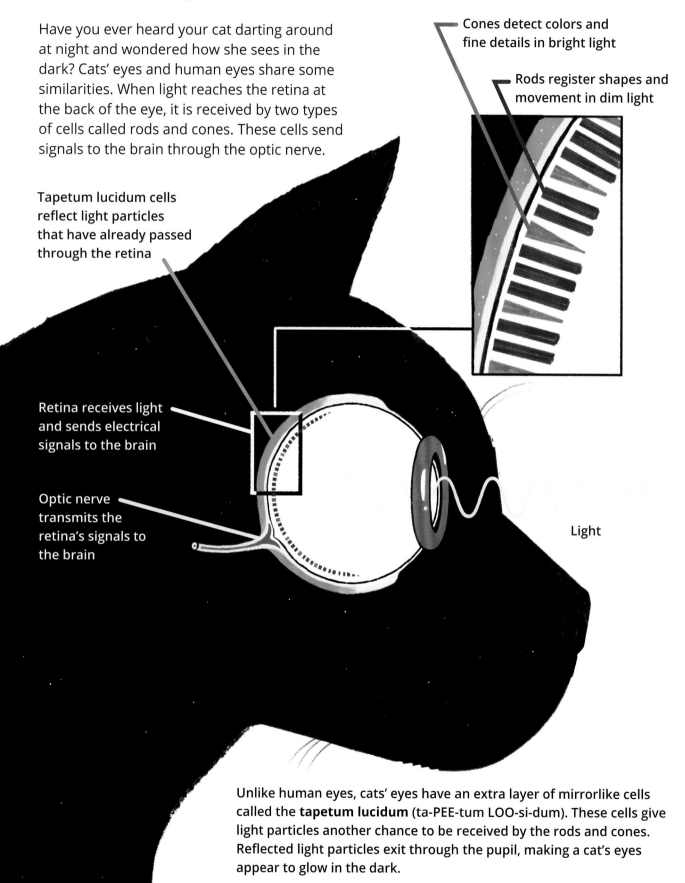

Retina receives light and sends electrical signals to the brain

Optic nerve transmits the retina's signals to the brain

Light

Unlike human eyes, cats' eyes have an extra layer of mirrorlike cells called the **tapetum lucidum** (ta-PEE-tum LOO-si-dum). These cells give light particles another chance to be received by the rods and cones. Reflected light particles exit through the pupil, making a cat's eyes appear to glow in the dark.

A CAT *Can See That!*

Cats' eyes have more rods and fewer cones than human eyes do, so a cat's vision will be less sharp at a distance than ours is in daylight. But at night, cats can see shapes and notice quick movements six to eight times better than humans can.

ENORMOUS *Eyes*

Imagine what you could see in the dark if each of your eyes were as big as a grapefruit! That's how big human eyes would be if we had the same eye-to-brain ratio as a tarsier. Tiny tarsiers have supersized eyes with wide pupils that let in as much light as possible.

But large eyes in a small head means less room for each eye to move, so tarsiers' eyes cannot rotate in their sockets. To get a good view, the tarsier rotates its whole head on its flexible neck. Some other nocturnal animals with big eyes, such as owls, also rotate their heads to see everything around them.

Night NOISES

Owls have adaptations other than big eyes — they also have specially adapted ears that help them navigate and hunt at night. Some species of owls have asymmetrical (uneven) ears. The ear opening on one side of the head is higher than the opening on the other side.

Owls move their heads from side to side, gathering sound information. All of these up and down, left and right signals combine instantly in the owl's brain to create a kind of map that pinpoints exactly where to find food. Owls also have a special arrangement of feathers around their faces. The feathers work like a satellite dish, collecting sound, amplifying it and directing it into the owl's ears.

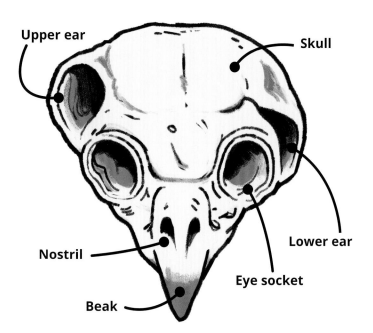

If a sound is louder in the upper ear, the owl knows its prey is flying above it.

If the prey is roaming below the owl, the sound will be louder in the owl's lower ear.

The owl also detects whether a sound is coming from the left or the right, depending on which ear it reaches first.

Echo, Echo, ECHOLOCATION

Like owls, bats are nocturnal. To navigate and find food in the dark, bats use a process called **echolocation**. They send out complicated patterns of sound waves from their mouths by moving air past their vibrating vocal chords. Some bats send out sound waves from their noses, where they have leaflike structures that act like megaphones. The sounds bats send out are so high-pitched that human ears can't hear them.

These sounds travel through the air and bounce off objects, creating echoes. Bats listen carefully to the echoes to collect information. Their brains use these details to figure out where possible prey is, as well as its size, speed and the direction it's moving.

FANCY FLAPS

Scientists believe that the different sizes, shapes, folds and wrinkles of a bat's outer ears all help to receive and direct sound.

(REALLY) GREAT HEARING

Did you know a great gray owl's hearing is so sharp it can hear a mouse moving as much as 60 cm (2 ft.) under the snow?

SSSSSSSSSMELLS *Good!*

How does a snake, slithering in the dark, sense where its next meal is? By using its forked tongue!

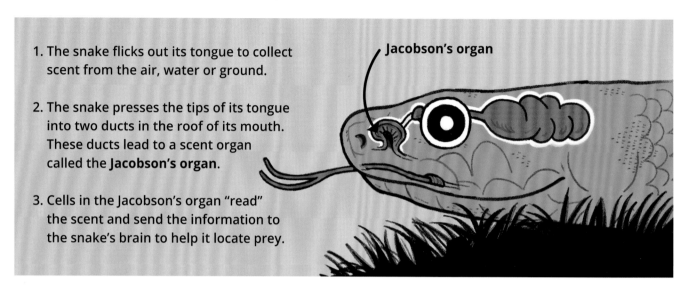

1. The snake flicks out its tongue to collect scent from the air, water or ground.

2. The snake presses the tips of its tongue into two ducts in the roof of its mouth. These ducts lead to a scent organ called the **Jacobson's organ**.

3. Cells in the Jacobson's organ "read" the scent and send the information to the snake's brain to help it locate prey.

Jacobson's organ

Why WHISKERS?

Ever notice that nocturnal mammals, such as rats, raccoons and red foxes, all have whiskers? Animals use these highly sensitive hairs to "feel" and gather clues from objects.

When whiskers brush against something, they vibrate. The vibrations are different depending on the size, shape and texture of the object. Nerve cells at the root of each whisker send information about these vibrations to the animal's brain, allowing the animal to better understand its environment, even in the dark.

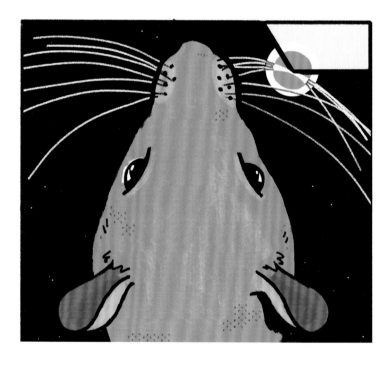

SENSIBLE!

Many nocturnal creatures combine information from several senses (vision, hearing, scent and vibration) to navigate, find prey and avoid danger at night.

Good VIBRATIONS

You might think nocturnal spiders, with their eight eyes, have excellent vision ... but the eyes of many spiders can detect only light and dark.

To sense even the smallest vibrations on their webs, spiders use their **lyriform organs**: groups of tiny parallel slits on their legs that are connected to nerve endings. These organs are so sensitive that a spider can tell the difference between a moth, a fly, a bee and another spider touching its web.

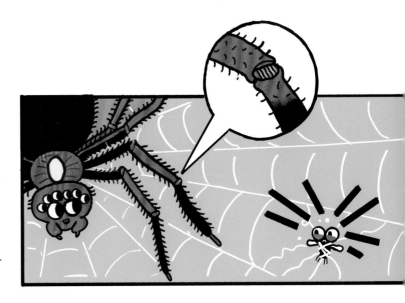

ASLEEP, WITH One Eye Open

Dolphins, seals, whales, manatees and some birds can be both awake *and* asleep — at once! This behavior is known as **unihemispheric** (YOO-nee-hem-iss-FEER-ic) **sleep**.

In dolphins, for example, one side of the brain rests while the other side stays alert, watching for predators and signaling when it's time to come up for air. The "asleep" and "alert" sides of the dolphin's brain alternate, so each side has a turn to rest. Whatever the alert side learns can even be transferred over to the other side of the brain.

Studies have shown that dolphins can remain awake in this way for at least 15 days straight, without any negative effects on their physical health or mental skills — easily beating Randy Gardner's world record.

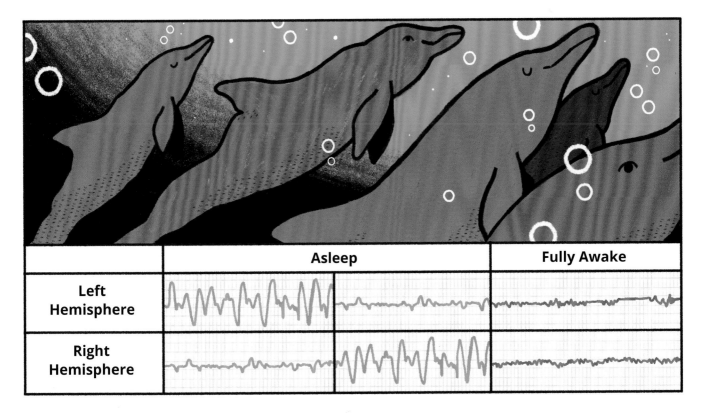

	Asleep		Fully Awake
Left Hemisphere	(active wave)	(flat wave)	(flat wave)
Right Hemisphere	(flat wave)	(active wave)	(flat wave)

WHEN LIGHT ISN'T *Right*

Like humans, nocturnal creatures have circadian rhythms. Darkness signals to their brains and bodies that it's time for them to wake, find food, build shelters and mate. But sometimes, **light pollution** interferes with these activities. Light pollution is unnatural brightness at night, caused by too many artificial lights. It can threaten nocturnal creatures' well-being and survival.

HOW CAN YOU HELP?

We need to think of our night sky as a valuable natural resource that needs conserving. Here are some things you can do to help prevent light pollution and its negative effects on nocturnal creatures:

- ✓ Encourage your family to turn off unnecessary lights at night.
- ✓ Write letters to businesses in your community to ask them to do the same.
- ✓ Ask your local government to choose energy-efficient street lighting that shines only downward.
- ✓ Raise money for organizations that work to protect nocturnal creatures.
- ✓ Talk to your friends and get them involved in these activities, too!

Moths and other insects are attracted to the lights humans leave on at night. Billions of them die this way each year.

Many snakes, salamanders and frogs are less active when there is a full moon, choosing instead to hunt or forage on darker nights when the chance of predators seeing them is lower. Light pollution can make every night seem like a full-moon night, and these creatures may not get enough to eat.

Birds such as warblers and sparrows navigate using the moon and stars. Brightly glowing cities confuse them and they may crash into buildings.

Fireflies rely on darkness to communicate with each other, using light flashes they create through a chemical reaction in their abdomens. Bright lights at night make it difficult for these winged beetles to detect each other's signals, attract mates and lure prey.

Sea turtles come to shore in the dark to lay their eggs, and the newly hatched babies need darkness to find their way to the sea. Too much artificial light discourages the females from laying eggs and lures the hatchlings away from the water, making them more likely to be caught by predators.

PLANT LIFE AT *Night*

In spring and summer, our natural environment is filled with green leaves and vibrant flowers, fruits and vegetables. But what does plant life look like after dark?

Like other living organisms, plants have a circadian rhythm. If you've ever seen a field of sunflowers slowly turning from east to west to follow the sun throughout the day, you've seen how a plant's internal clock works.

The stems, leaves and flowers of plants all have cells containing **phytochromes** (FY-tuh-crohms), tiny molecules that are sensitive to light. Phytochromes detect whether it is day or night and use this information to set off chemical reactions within the plant to help it grow and develop.

Phytochromes

DO PLANTS *Sleep?*

Plants don't sleep at night in the same way humans do. But in response to darkness, many of them close their flowers, or droop or fold their leaves at dusk. This type of movement is known as **nyctinasty** (NICK-ti-nas-tee).

Though scientists are not yet sure why some plants have evolved to behave this way at night, they do have some hypotheses.

Plants that close their blooms or droop their branches after dark may be conserving energy. In daytime, they need to reach upward to collect sunlight and attract insects for pollination.

Other plants may close their flowers to protect pollen from becoming soggy with dew. Dry pollen is more likely to stick to insects and be carried to other plants for pollination.

When it's dark, some plants may fold up their leaves to play defense against nocturnal predators. It's harder for scurrying ground critters to eat a closed plant.

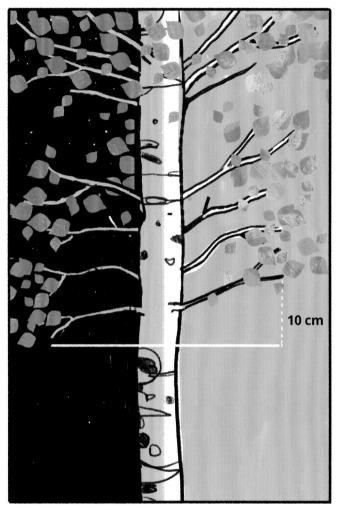

10 cm

Birch trees relax the tips of all their branches at night, making them droop as much as 10 cm (4 in.)! The branches begin returning to their regular daytime position before sunrise.

Poppies close their flowers at night using changes in water pressure. The plant responds to darkness by pumping water out of the cells at the base of its petals, causing them to fold inward.

Green ENERGY

We need to eat food to stay active and healthy. Because plants are living organisms, they, too, have food and energy needs. But plants can't get a snack from the kitchen. They rely on two internal energy processes: **photosynthesis**, to produce food, and **cellular respiration**, to break down that food and release energy.

During daylight, plants perform both photosynthesis *and* cellular respiration. At night, when there is no sunlight, photosynthesis is not possible. Plants perform cellular respiration around the clock, though, releasing energy for themselves even when it's dark outside.

2 Plants absorb energy from sunlight and carbon dioxide from the air.

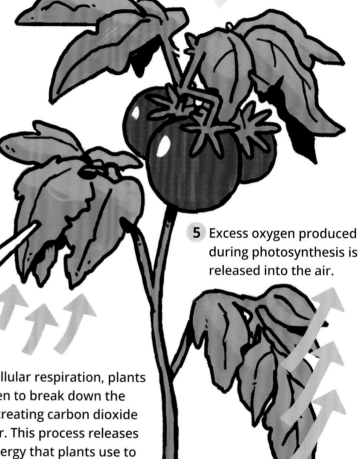

1 Photosynthesis takes place in **chloroplasts**, tiny structures in a plant's leaf cells. Chloroplasts contain molecules of chlorophyll (KLOR-uh-fill), a green pigment that absorbs sunlight.

5 Excess oxygen produced during photosynthesis is released into the air.

4 During cellular respiration, plants use oxygen to break down the glucose, creating carbon dioxide and water. This process releases stored energy that plants use to grow, form flowers and develop fruits and vegetables.

3 Plants combine water from the ground with the sunlight and carbon dioxide to create oxygen and glucose (a kind of sugar). Glucose is the plant's food.

PLANT *Math*

At night, plants are faced with a dilemma: How do they use the energy they stored up during photosynthesis in just the right way, so that they don't run out before the sun rises?

Scientists have found that plants are pretty good at math! Using chemical processes inside their leaves, plants measure how much sugar they have saved and estimate how much time there is until dawn. They divide their amount of stored energy by the number of hours in the night, figuring out exactly how quickly or slowly they should use their sugar.

The math plants do is so precise that by sunrise, they will always have only a small amount of their stored energy left over. These automatic calculations prevent plants from starving or stopping growth overnight.

MOON *Gardens*

If you've ever been in a garden on a sunny afternoon, you've probably seen brightly colored flowers attracting daytime pollinators. But have you ever taken a walk in a moon garden, specially planted to be enjoyed at night?

Some plants have adapted to attract nocturnal pollinators like bats and moths. These plants wait until after dark to open their white or pale flowers, which glow under the moonlight. Many of these nocturnal blooms also have a strong scent.

Evening primrose flowers open around sunset and last for only one night. The pollen is designed to stick well to its main pollinators, nocturnal sphinx moths.

Moonflowers have large, silky flowers that grow on a vine and open quickly in the evening, releasing a heavy fragrance.

Night phlox is also known as "midnight candy" because its blooms have a sweet scent.

Night-blooming jasmine has a powerful scent that its nighttime pollinators can detect from miles away. This shrub's flowers open after dark.

What's That SMELL?!

One of the world's smelliest plants is the **titan arum** (a.k.a. "corpse flower"). Taller than an adult human, this giant plant blooms once every few years. Its flower gives off a horrible stink that is strongest at night — think rotten steak, old fish, the bottom of a dumpster and sweaty feet! The scent attracts nocturnal beetles that like to lay their eggs in decaying animal flesh. Tricked by the smell, the beetles transfer pollen as they move from plant to plant.

Beetle

NIGHT GIANT

The giant water lily's white flower is about the size of a soccer ball and opens only at night. This flower gives off heat and a strong pineapple scent, which attracts scarab beetles for pollination.

QUEEN OF THE NIGHT

The night-blooming cereus, known as "queen of the night," is a desert cactus plant that looks like a cluster of dry, bare stems most of the time. For one summer night each year, the plant reveals a sweet but short surprise: a large, beautifully scented white flower that wilts before sunrise.

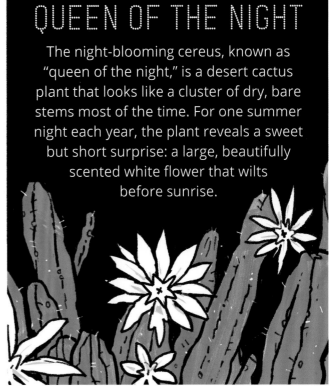

THE Night Sky

There are many glowing objects in our sky that aren't visible in daylight, when the sun outshines them. If you know when and where to look after dark, you can find stars, comets, meteors and more with just your own eyes.

WHY IS THERE Night?

Our lives revolve around a very predictable pattern of day and night, light and darkness. But why exactly does this pattern happen? Earth is like a spinning top that never stops turning. Every 24 hours, our planet completes one full rotation by spinning from west to east on its axis, an imaginary straight line running through its center. As it rotates, Earth is also orbiting the sun. The sun's light shines on only one side of Earth at a time. Because Earth is constantly rotating on its axis, the light side and the dark side keep shifting, creating the cycle of day and night.

TILT-A-WHIRL

Different places on Earth experience days and nights of different lengths. Because Earth's axis is tilted by about 23.5 degrees, one hemisphere tilts just a little more toward the sun, while the other leans a little more away. As Earth revolves around the sun, each hemisphere gets a turn to experience the longer, warmer days of summer and the shorter, cooler days of winter.

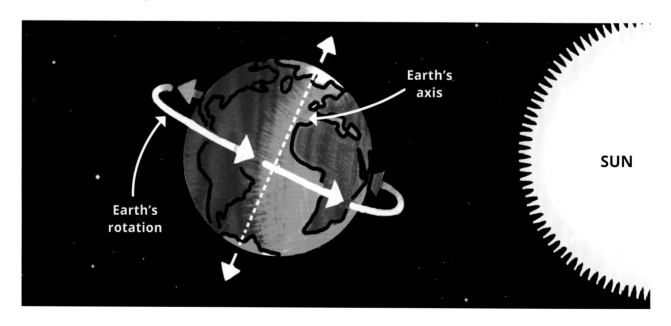

Earth's axis

Earth's rotation

SUN

Midnight Sun
AND POLAR NIGHT

Did you know that during certain parts of the year in Earth's polar regions, light or darkness can last all 24 hours of the day? When at least part of the sun is always visible, it's known as "**midnight sun**." The term "**polar night**" describes periods when the sun doesn't rise above the horizon at all.

During Northern Hemisphere summers, periods of midnight sun occur in parts of Norway, Alaska, Canada, Russia, Greenland and Finland. Midnight sun also occurs in Antarctica in Southern Hemisphere summers. In winter, these same places experience polar nights. It can be difficult for people in these regions to get the right amount of sleep, since their brains and bodies don't receive the usual natural cues of light and darkness.

Midnight Sun

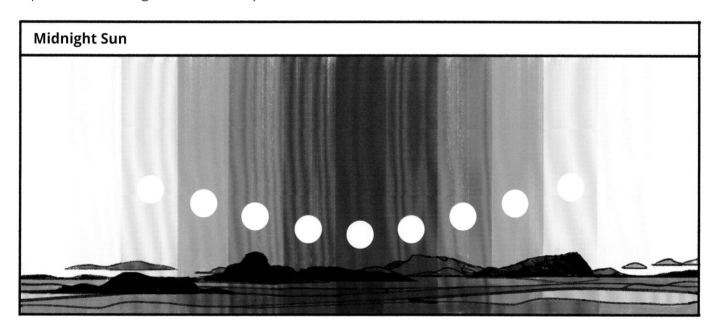

Polar Night

STAR LIGHT, *Star Bright*

On a clear, moonless night, away from city lights, our eyes can see about two thousand to twenty-five hundred stars (a small fraction of the many billions of stars in our galaxy!). Stars usually appear white to us because our eyes collect just a tiny amount of the light they give off. But stars emit light in a whole rainbow of colors.

Stars look tiny to our eyes, but they are giant balls of gas held together by their own gravity. They shine because they produce energy through a process called **fusion**. The temperature and pressure in the core of most stars are so high that hydrogen atoms combine and form helium. The heat and light energy created by fusion radiates out into space.

Brilliant!

Many people believe the brightest star in the sky is Polaris (a.k.a. the North Star), but Sirius is actually the most brilliant star visible from Earth. This white-blue star appears to twinkle with many colors. At 8.6 **light years** away, Sirius is one of the closest stars to us.

Polaris is farther away from Earth than Sirius and is only a medium-bright star, but we can still see it clearly. In the Northern Hemisphere, Polaris is visible at the end of the handle of the Little Dipper, signaling where due north is. This star has long been an important navigation tool for humans and birds. To us, Polaris looks like a single point of light, but it is really a system of three stars.

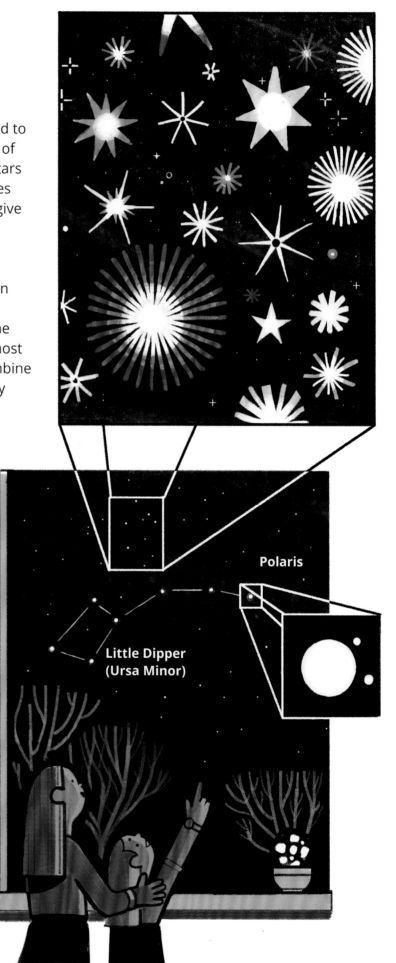

Polaris

Little Dipper (Ursa Minor)

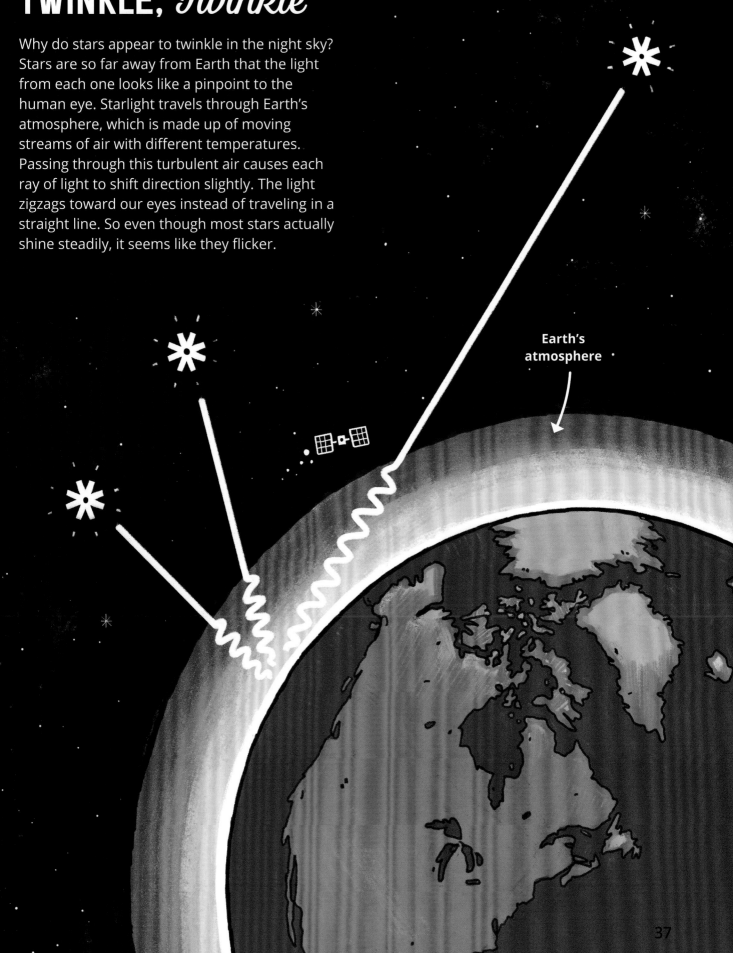

TWINKLE, *Twinkle*

Why do stars appear to twinkle in the night sky? Stars are so far away from Earth that the light from each one looks like a pinpoint to the human eye. Starlight travels through Earth's atmosphere, which is made up of moving streams of air with different temperatures. Passing through this turbulent air causes each ray of light to shift direction slightly. The light zigzags toward our eyes instead of traveling in a straight line. So even though most stars actually shine steadily, it seems like they flicker.

Earth's atmosphere

Pictures and PATTERNS

Do you see pictures when you look up at the stars? Maybe you've found **constellations** like Ursa Major, Ursa Minor, Orion and Cassiopeia. In total, there are 88 officially recognized constellations. Each one has a name and forms a particular shape or pattern in the night sky.

Constellations were created by humans with good imaginations, not by nature. People long ago used the stars to navigate, to know when seasons were changing or to tell important stories. They grouped stars into pictures they could use to "read" the night sky. But the stars in a constellation are usually tens, hundreds or even thousands of light years apart from each other!

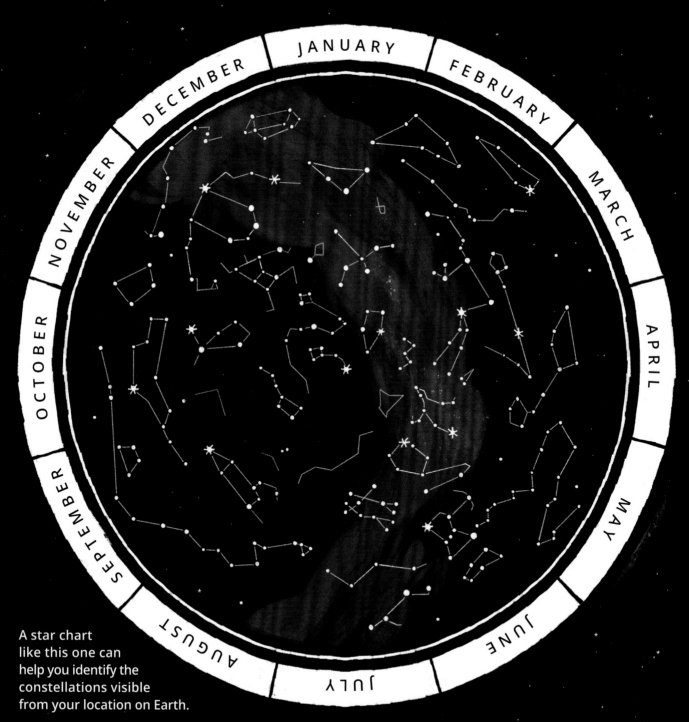

A star chart like this one can help you identify the constellations visible from your location on Earth.

POSITIVELY *Planets*

Stars are not the only bright objects in our night sky — planets also appear regularly. Planets don't create their own light, but they do reflect the sun's light, making it possible for us to see them. If you know where and when to look, you can find some planets with just your eyes.

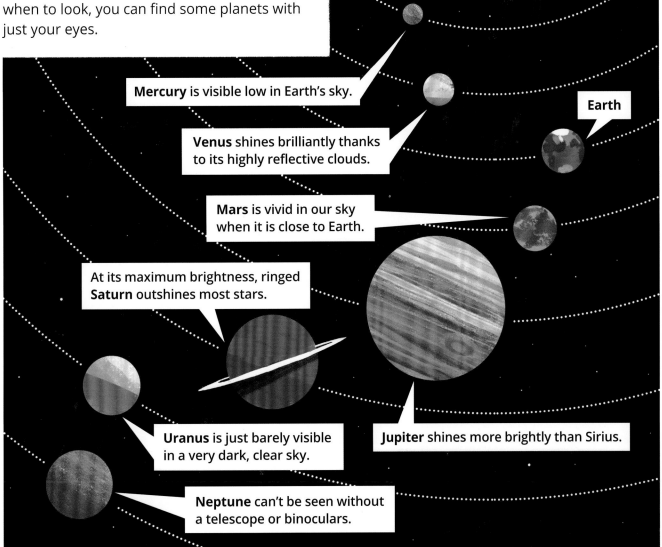

SUN

Mercury is visible low in Earth's sky.

Venus shines brilliantly thanks to its highly reflective clouds.

Earth

Mars is vivid in our sky when it is close to Earth.

At its maximum brightness, ringed **Saturn** outshines most stars.

Uranus is just barely visible in a very dark, clear sky.

Jupiter shines more brightly than Sirius.

Neptune can't be seen without a telescope or binoculars.

A STEADY SHINE

Usually, planets shine steadily in the night sky, rather than appearing to twinkle like stars do. They're closer to Earth than the stars, so each planet looks like a tiny disk of light instead of a pinpoint. As a planet's reflected sunlight travels through Earth's atmosphere, the zigs and zags of the many light points cancel each other out, and we see a steady light.

THE MOON'S *Many Moods*

You've seen the moon with its face sometimes full and round and sometimes winking in a crescent-shaped sliver. Why does the moon's shape appear to change?

Like planets, the moon glows because its surface reflects the sun's light. Only the side of the moon facing the sun is lit up. Every 27.3 days, the moon completes one full rotation on its axis, creating its own cycle of day and night. It also orbits once around Earth. We see different amounts of the moon's lit side, also known as different phases of the moon.

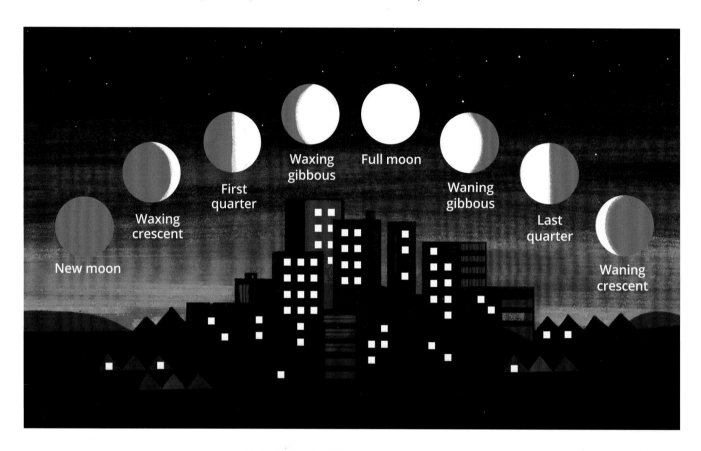

New moon

Waxing crescent

First quarter

Waxing gibbous

Full moon

Waning gibbous

Last quarter

Waning crescent

SPIN CYCLE

The moon's rate of spin on its axis exactly matches its rate of orbit around Earth. No matter which phase the moon is in, or what season it is, we always see the same side of the moon.

MOON *Illusion*

Have you noticed the moon looks bigger and brighter when it's lower in the sky than it does when it's higher? This is an optical illusion — the moon doesn't actually change size. Scientists aren't sure why a low-hanging moon looks larger to us. One possible explanation is the illusion on the right, discovered by German psychologist Hermann Ebbinghaus in the 1800s. Which middle circle is bigger?

Both middle circles are the same size! But the one above *looks* bigger because the sizes of the black circles influence our perception. When the moon is low in the sky, it may appear huge because of the trees, mountains and buildings in sight nearby. But when the moon is higher, surrounded by the vastness of space, it seems smaller.

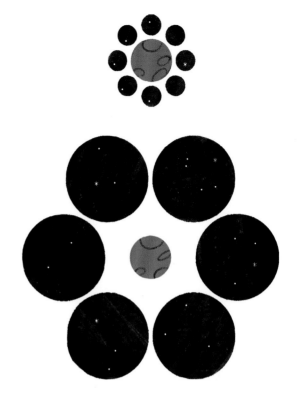

ECLIPSES EXPLAINED

Occasionally, when the moon is full, we might see an eclipse. **Lunar eclipses** happen when the sun, Earth and moon are positioned in a straight or almost straight line. Earth blocks direct sunlight from reaching the moon, and Earth's shadow covers all or part of the moon's face. The moon can appear to have a reddish glow during a total eclipse. Sunlight streams around Earth and is filtered and bent by Earth's atmosphere, indirectly lighting up the moon's surface.

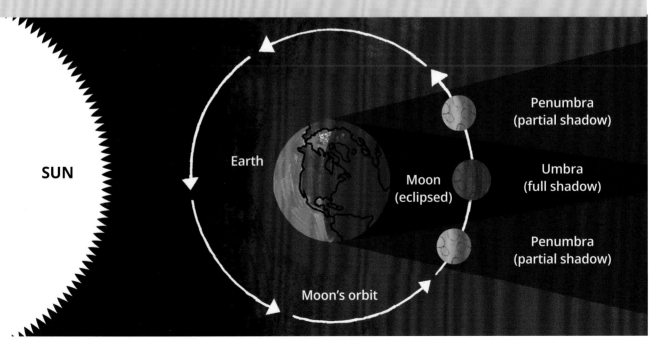

SUN

Earth

Moon (eclipsed)

Moon's orbit

Penumbra (partial shadow)

Umbra (full shadow)

Penumbra (partial shadow)

Cool COMETS

In the chilly outer regions of our solar system, billions of **comets** orbit the sun. Comets are icy bodies made up of gases, rock and dust leftover from the formation of the sun and planets 4.6 billion years ago. Occasionally, bright comets appear in our night sky, creating a spectacular light show.

When a comet's orbit passes near the sun, the comet heats up and some of its icy surface vaporizes. This creates a halo, or coma, of evaporated gas and dust surrounding the frozen center, or nucleus, of the comet. Streams of energetic particles from the sun push the gas and dust away from the comet, resulting in glowing tails that can stretch for hundreds of millions of kilometers (miles)!

New comets are discovered each year and are usually named after the person or spacecraft who found them.

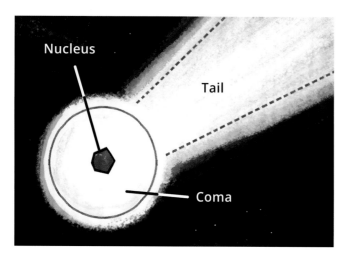

What a TRIP!

Comets that take fewer than two hundred years to orbit the sun are called short-period comets. They come from the Kuiper (KYE-per) Belt, an area of the solar system just past Neptune's orbit. Other comets can take up to 30 million years to finish one trip around the sun! These long-period comets come from the Oort Cloud, a giant shell of icy debris surrounding our solar system.

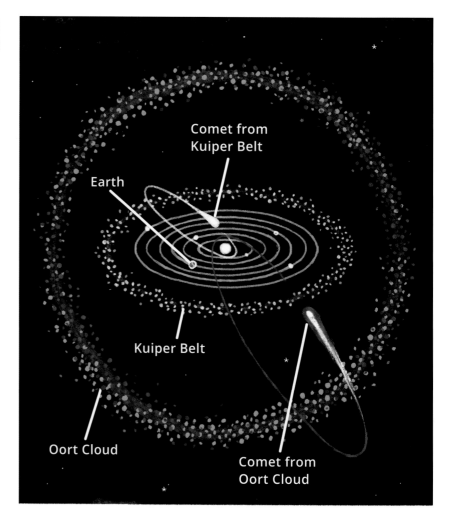

METEOR *Magic*

Have you ever seen a shooting star? What you noticed was actually a **meteor**: a bit of space rock falling through Earth's atmosphere. As these rocks streak across the sky, they create friction with the gases in the atmosphere. The friction is so great that the rock gives off a trail of light.

On a clear, moonless night away from city lights, it's possible to see several meteors per hour. We might see many more during a meteor shower, which can happen when Earth travels through the path of dust particles left behind by a comet or an asteroid. Because Earth crosses the orbits of certain comets and asteroids on the same dates each year, astronomers can predict the best meteor-watching nights.

Meteor Stream	Peak Nights*	Number of Meteors per Hour
Quadrantids	January 3–4	60–200
Lyrids	April 21–22	10–15
Eta Aquarids	May 5–6	40–85
Delta Aquariids	July 27–28	15–20
Perseids	August 11–12	60–100
Orionids	October 20–21	25
Leonids	November 17–18	10–15
Geminids	December 13–14	60–120

* may vary by +/- one day

Amazing AURORAS

The dancing lights of the **auroras** are one of nature's most colorful nighttime displays. Also known as the northern and southern lights, the auroras shimmer across dark skies in shades of pink, green, yellow, blue and violet. But how do they happen?

The sun releases electrically charged particles into space, both in a steady stream, called solar wind, and in giant, powerful bursts called solar flares. Earth's invisible magnetic field bounces most of these particles away. Some particles do reach Earth and are attracted to the north and south magnetic poles. When these particles strike oxygen and nitrogen molecules in Earth's atmosphere, the molecules emit light, a reaction known as the aurora borealis (northern lights) and aurora australis (southern lights).

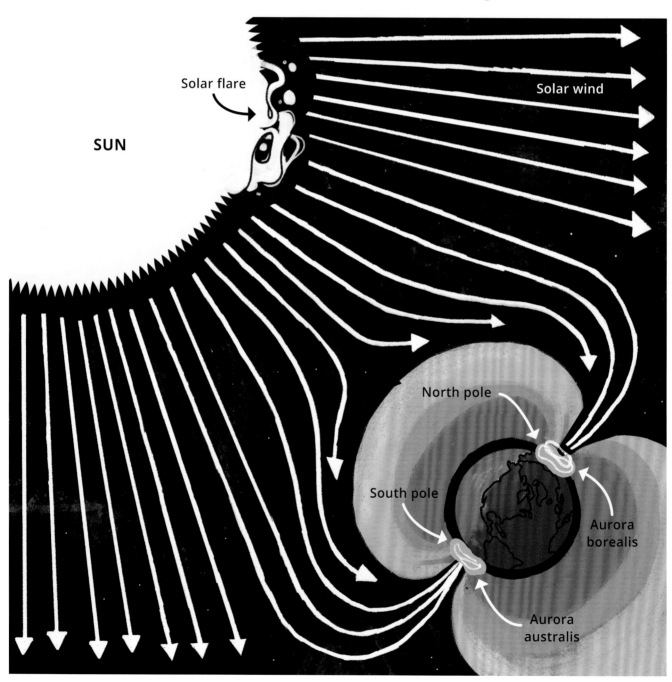

Solar flare

Solar wind

SUN

North pole

South pole

Aurora borealis

Aurora australis

Bright SPOTS

Solar wind creates auroras almost every night. But during solar storms, when the sun is especially active, the auroras can be brilliant and spectacular. Winter nights give the best conditions for viewing them, thanks to more hours of darkness and crisper, clearer winter air.

The best spots to watch the northern lights are in Alaska, northern Canada, Norway, Sweden, Finland, Iceland and Greenland. The southern lights happen over Antarctica, but they can sometimes be seen in southern Australia and New Zealand.

LAST Thoughts BEFORE BED ...

When we close our eyes and drift off, the world is not simply dark and quiet — it hums with life. Our brains clean themselves, dream and process information. Our bodies release hormones, repair tissues, shift and snore. Nocturnal creatures of all kinds move about searching for food, building shelters and finding mates. Plants break down sugars overnight so they can grow, and some of them bloom beautifully after dark. Up in the night sky, objects in our solar system spin, orbit, stream and fall, creating or reflecting light that shines toward us.

The night still holds many mysteries about the wild and wonderful things that happen while we sleep. Maybe that's something *you* can dream about.

GLOSSARY

adaptation: a genetic change, passed down from one generation to the next, that helps an organism survive in its environment

auroras: shimmering, colored lights in the sky, created when electrically charged particles from the sun interact with gas molecules in Earth's atmosphere. Also known as the northern and southern lights.

cellular respiration: a process in which plants use oxygen to break down glucose, creating carbon dioxide and water. Plants use the energy freed during this process to grow and develop.

chloroplasts: tiny structures in a plant's leaf cells where photosynthesis occurs

circadian rhythm: a natural 24-hour cycle of sleeping and waking, driven by an organism's internal clock in response to environmental cues such as light and temperature

comet: an icy body from the outer regions of our solar system made up of gases, rock and dust left over from the formation of the sun and planets

constellation: a grouping of stars that has a name and forms a particular shape or pattern in the night sky

crepuscular: active during twilight hours, just after the sun rises and just before the sun sets

diurnal: active during the day

echolocation: a process that some creatures, such as bats, use to navigate and locate prey by emitting sound waves and listening for the echoes that bounce back from objects

fusion: a process that happens in a star's core, where extremely high temperatures and pressure cause hydrogen atoms to combine and form helium. The heat and light created by fusion radiate out into space.

hormones: chemical substances in the bodies of living things that control what certain cells or organs do

Jacobson's organ: a scent organ found in the roof of the mouth of some creatures, such as snakes

light pollution: unnatural brightness at night caused by the use of too many artificial lights, which can have harmful effects on humans and wildlife

light year: the distance a beam of light travels in one Earth year, or about 9.5 trillion km (5.9 trillion mi.)

limbic system: a set of connected structures in the brain that are involved in our emotions, memories and motivations

lunar eclipse: when Earth blocks direct sunlight from reaching the moon, and Earth's shadow covers all or part of the moon's face. A lunar eclipse occurs when the sun, Earth and moon are positioned in a straight or almost straight line.

lyriform organ: a highly sensitive organ found in the legs of spiders, made up of tiny parallel slits that detect web vibrations

meteor: a bit of space rock falling through Earth's atmosphere that appears in the sky as a streak of light because of friction

midnight sun: a natural event that occurs when at least part of the sun is always visible during a 24-hour period. It occurs in summer in Earth's polar regions.

nocturnal: active at night

nyctinasty: movements that a plant makes in response to darkness, such as closing its flowers, or drooping or folding its leaves

photosynthesis: a process in which a plant uses light energy from the sun, water from the ground and carbon dioxide from the air to create glucose and oxygen

phytochromes: tiny, light-sensitive molecules in the cells of a plant's stems, leaves and flowers that detect whether it is day or night

polar night: a natural event that occurs when the sun does not rise above the horizon at all during a 24-hour period. It occurs in winter in Earth's polar regions.

prefrontal cortex: a set of connected structures in the brain that are involved in problem solving, planning and reasoning

somnambulism: the scientific term for sleepwalking

suprachiasmatic nucleus: a group of nerve cells in the brain that coordinate the timing of important body tasks like eating and sleeping

tapetum lucidum: an extra layer of mirrorlike cells in the eyes of some nocturnal creatures. These cells reflect light back through the retina.

titan arum: a giant plant, also known as "corpse flower," that blooms only once every few years and releases a horrible stink when it does

unihemispheric sleep: a type of sleep seen in some birds and aquatic mammals in which one half of the brain rests while the other half stays alert

SELECTED *Sources*

Dickinson, Terence. *Nightwatch: A Practical Guide to Viewing the Universe*. 4th ed. Richmond Hill: Firefly Books, 2008.

Healthy Sleep. Harvard Medical School, Division of Sleep Medicine and WGBH Educational Foundation, 2008. htttp://www .healthysleep.med.harvard.edu/healthy/.

NASA Science: Solar System Exploration. NASA. https://solarsystem.nasa.gov/.

Nocturnal animals. DKfindout!, 2019. https:// www.dkfindout.com/uk/animals-and-nature/ nocturnal-animals/.

"Nocturnal Animals at Woodland Park Zoo: Pre-Visit Information for Teachers." Woodland Park Zoo, 2010. https://www.zoo .org/Document.Doc?id=75.

Savage, Dasha. "How Plants Tell Time - Dasha Savage." TED-Ed. https://ed.ted.com/lessons/ how-plants-tell-time-dasha-savage.

Semple, Jeff, dir. *The Nature of Things: While You Were Sleeping*. Infield Fly Productions for CBC, 2016. www.cbc.ca/natureofthings/ episodes/while-your-were-sleeping.

Space. EarthSky. https://earthsky.org/space.

Stickgold, Robert. "Sleep, Memory, and Dreams - Robert Stickgold, PhD." BostonMOS. November 20, 2014, YouTube video, 1:32:17. https://www.youtube.com/ watch?v=XUA3fL4mzhg.

Stöckl, Anna. "How do animals see in the dark? - Anna Stöckl." TED-Ed. August 25, 2016, YouTube video, 4:22. https://www.youtube.com/ watch?v=t3CjTU7TaNA&feature=youtu.be.

Index